This book is dedicated to my grade 12
Writer's Craft teacher, Mrs. Siegel.

Without her, I'd never have the courage
to write it all down.

Introduction

I went down to the river
one last time to set myself free

while I bathed, I shed the pain
                      sadness
                      hurt

that had grown into me
over the past fifteen years
like a second layer
of skin

I've been having difficulty
finding balance lately,
but I think my roots
are finally starting
to grow

and from those roots
sprouted branches

I think I'm finally
coming clean

sowing

you made me feel
like I was hard to love

and I will never
forgive you
for that

touch me
pull my hair back
make me scream

I want to know what it's like
I want to feel real again

realizations I made when I was high

I am an earthquake
I am an earthquake
I am an earthquake

sex
was a transaction

I paid for comfort
in sloppy kisses
and bruised thighs

and wondered why
I could possibly feel
this empty

lying beneath someone
trying to fill
so much space

you're still under my skin
still breaking my bones
still making a home
out of my ribcage

Your hand is still wrapped
around my throat
still squeezing it shut
but it doesn't hurt anymore

I keep telling myself that
it doesn't hurt anymore

to all the boys
who made the bed shake
but never my thighs:

you made me feel like
a car crash

a pair of legs
broken
so that you could fit
between them

when I was fourteen
I thought if I could make
my hipbones and ribcage
protrude through my skin
like mountains beside a valley

someone might want me enough
to consider me their world

he scraped my insides out
like a cantaloupe

and had the nerve
to ask me
if I liked it

I used to be yours
but now you look at me
like I'm a crime scene

so I guess I really am
still yours

so if all you want out of this
is to put your hands on me
can we pretend that this is love?

can we pretend that
I'm not this empty shell
that only feels whole
when you touch me?

I'd let you choke me
if it meant I got to feel your arms
around me

I'll pretend the bruises
are hickies
if it means
I get to see you again

you loved me
like you loved
a ghost town

and like a ghost town
I never learned
how to let go
of anyone
who has ever
lived inside me

I tore parts of myself
out

to keep you
whole

vomit:

      morning sickness
      alcohol poisoning
      hangover
      cried too hard
      nervousness
      the flu
      acid reflux
      food poisoning
      ate too much
      took too many
      and
      decided to stay

I guess you can tell a lot
about a person
by the way
their body chooses
to get rid of
the bad stuff

I'm only ever
a convenient body
with weak knees and
a warm heart

no one
has ever wanted me
whole

peel off my clothes
hold me down to the bed
make a home out of my body
leave as quickly as you came

when the pills were done
hollowing out your body

they got your head
too

addiction

the temptation
will wrap itself
so tightly
around your throat

that you can't take a breath
without thinking about it

when my life fell to pieces
I looked for answers
in bent back spoons

I guess you can keep me

and every piece you left
bleeding in the streets

today I saw a flower
covered in snow
and I cried

I wondered what it was like
to be buried alive

rooting

the past
like a boomerang

always
comes back

the first night in inpatient treatment

this bed is not a grave:
you are here to heal

<u>an apology letter to the person I was this summer</u>

this is just to say
that I am sorry
for the way I treated you

and how I made you do things
that you really
didn't want to do.

so I promise
that you will never have to swallow
another mouthful
of anything
that makes you feel empty

and I will never
make you take your clothes off
for anyone
who wants nothing more
than a vacation
out of you

is the opposite
of a pregnancy

when the body caves in
on itself?

some memories
soften

and some just
burn

you still feel like home
even with the walls caved in

and all the furniture gone

from a very young age
I was taught that the word *love*
was a word
that I would never be able to swallow
no matter how many times
it was spat at me

so forgive me, because
whenever someone tells me
they love me
I have to brace myself
for the impact

remember the good days
hold on to them tightly,
but do not let them suffocate

remember the bad days
and like a dry pill stuck

to the back of your throat,
do whatever it takes
to swallow them

dear Mom,

you don't know me
you never did
and never will

love,
    me, I guess

I can't tell my parents
I'm a boy

but maybe
if I bind my chest
and wear ill-fitting pants
they'll get the idea

I'm terrified that
I'm not living fast enough

I've spent the majority of my life miserable
and it's slipping away
too quickly for me to keep up

I'm scared that someday
I'm going to end up on my deathbed
and realize that I've been a ghost
the whole time

I wish I could tell you
what it was like
to live in a house where the walls
caved in on themselves
every night
and rebuilt themselves
every morning

but I am still learning
to pull the stones
out from under my tongue
and not be ashamed
when I get blood on the mattress

so please be patient
when I say
I am scared to go home

I always tell people
it's cause it's haunted
because I can't
find the words to explain
that it's not the ghosts
I'm afraid of

I spent the majority of my youth drunk
and miserable on my bedroom floor
pretending that these were
the best years of my life

I've been holding myself back
for so long

and I don't know what I'm scared of
I don't know what I'm hiding from

I'm at this really awkward
stage in my life
where it feels like I'm a person
but I'm not quite there yet

my childhood was
learning that home
is not the only place
that love
comes from

my childhood was
biting into lollipops
and holding my tongue

I guess this is growing up

the way we get used to pulling teeth
from our stomachs

and thinking we'd be better off
falling asleep with the stars

my problem is that
whenever I feel good

it's never for the right reasons

borderline personality disorder
===

every emotion I've ever felt
has always been some variation
of painful

I was thinking about the last time
I felt this hopeless:

sixteen behind the wheel
of my mother's car
wondering what would happen
if I closed my eyes

I didn't
so I slept with the lights on that night
and wondered how
an artificial light
could emit so much warmth

I did everything I could
to feel real again

and I think that
was my biggest mistake

I am an ashtray
for the person I used to be

I am not afraid of feeling pain
what I'm afraid of
is it never going away

your past turns to dust
inside you

this is where
ghosts come from

this is how they learn
to haunt you

I keep to myself
most of the time

I still think about you,

                                          but not like I used to

my heartbeat
is a time-bomb

I don't know how
they expect me to survive

with a heart that's trying to
eat me alive

there's something about the way
you said

    "goodnight"

like when you closed your eyes
I watched the sun set
behind them
and I knew
I would never see it again

there are cities
burning
inside me

the world is too much for me
to face
with bleeding lips

sprouting

I am still learning
to have wounds

but not think of them
as wounds

it hurts to leave
but I'm afraid
that if I don't go now
I might suffocate
in here

maybe sometimes
we have to break
our own hearts

   maybe
   the only way out of this

is to crack the seed
all the way open
and grow from it

people need homes
and like an empty space

I needed you

open up your ribcage
let me see your heart

I will pull the strings apart
I will get the tangles out

I am a storm
with soft skin

the kind that makes
houses tremble
from within

you caught raindrops
on your tongue
like God was begging you
to taste him

being in love
with your roommate
sucks

but at least
I get to hear her masturbate
through the wall

hold me down on the bed

tell me that I look pretty
in the sunlight

I want to know what it's like
to wake up in the morning
with our thighs
still stuck together

I'm not the best human
but I've got good intentions
and the heart to prove it

dear Trump,

I am tired
and heartbroken

and now I will love
louder
and harder
than ever

allow everything
to make you tender

even the knives twisted
in your stomach

sometimes childhood
is not linear

there are still nights when
I curl up in bed and I'm back
where I started:

in cars, in fields,
in places far away from here
but not far enough

I have grown
and been plucked

and I still ache
for the hands
that pulled me

there is a soft kind of
love
inside me

the quiet kind
the trembling kind

the most beautiful moments
I've spent in this life
are the days with you
lying in bed
talking quietly
of the world
spinning around us

I didn't realize
how much I loved you
until I felt you
in my veins

but to call you a knife
doesn't even begin to describe
how bad it hurt
when you left

I think my heart's gone missing
I keep hearing it beat
from miles away

you must have taken it
with you
when you said goodbye

I want to be more
than just your best friend

I want to run my hands
through the tangles in your hair
and show you that love
is never a word you have to say
through clenched teeth

I want you to know
that you are so much more
than the quiet, uneven beat
of your feeble heart

every wish I've ever spent
on a shooting star
has been about you

and how all I want
is for you to be anything
but this fleeting moment of light

growing

sometimes
when I see a streetlight
I mistake it
for the moon

and I think
I do the same thing
when I look at you

my heart is filling up
again

and this time
it's only
for me

I have ripened
and now it is time
for me to love
and love
and love

I tattooed the words
"brave boy"
on my thigh

because all my life
I have been told
that I am neither

let the dust collect
on your heart

let flowers
grow from it

together
we were a wildfire

and for that
I am sorry

I hope you never make a home
out of someone who makes you feel
like you're burning
to the ground

we must protect this world
and all of its beautiful
beating hearts

you were the coffee stains
I couldn't scrub off
my bedside table

and like my morning
caffeine halo
I'm addicted to you

I want to be
your cemetery

the place where you
lay to rest

all the bodies
that came before me

I think there are flowers
growing
from where you
planted kisses

tell me
about how I became
your favourite name
to moan

it snowed
the night you left

I guess we kept
the city warm

catharsis is
inhaling each other's breath
before falling asleep

have you ever
kissed a ghost
        my love?

have you ever
felt the cold breeze
on your tongue

that made it feel like
you were floating away?

blooming

I've loved
I've lost

I'm all
that I've got

the way sunlight
touches your face

is its own genre
of poetry

I am allowed to have green hair
I will cry when I'm upset
I won't let him keep kissing me
I will finish my homework
I will call my mother on her birthday
I will not stay up past midnight
I will not forget to lock the door
I will eat my vegetables
I am allowed to still be in pieces
I am allowed to let it hurt
I am allowed to be afraid
I am allowed to be loved

I swear I didn't use to be
this cold

I'm still healing
and it's just a lot

      It's just a lot

forgive yourself
for his
watered down love

it isn't your fault
you weren't
able to bloom

losing you
hurt

but at least
I got myself
back

I wanna know how soft
you can be
between my thighs

by the time you're done,
I don't want there to be
any honey left

keep the sweaters
I gave you

I don't need them
to keep me warm
anymore

my life is full
of accomplishments

for example:
I have lived
and lived
and lived

the inpatient perspective

now I know what it's like
to be a butterfly
trapped in a mason jar
without any holes
in it

keep the poems
I wrote for you
I don't want them back

keep the heart
I carved out for you, too
I don't want that
either

you will burn
and you will burn brightly

like a candle
your excess wax
will melt away

and like a phoenix
you will be born
again

falling in love with a trauma survivor is not easy

give her a chance
to melt

give her a chance
to get used to
being warm again

the streetlights
that turn on at night
on the walk back home
greet me
like an old friend

I want to know
if you've ever been warm
for longer than
the summer

if you've ever felt the sun
on your skin
and knew it was safe
to wrap your fingers
around it, and let it in

you've got veins
that look like a road map

when the doctors asked you
where it hurts
you had to strip down
and show them:

    "here
    and here"

you pulled your ribcage apart
and showed them
your beating heart
and said

    "everything that hurts
    seems to start from here"

this world is not
the product
of some kind and forgiving god

and my body is not
the product
of some kind of
flesh and blood romance

pour me out

I want to be empty
I want to start over

at the end of it all,
I took a deep breath in

and listened to my faint
but trying
heartbeat:

   I am still here
                            still here
                            still here

About the Author

Andy Gardiner is a non-binary writer and artist living in Toronto and Kingston ON, currently working on their English degree in preparation for law school. *From the Roots* is their first full-length book of poetry, although they have published small batches of zines in the past.

From the Roots is a small collection of poems that tell a story of regrowth starting at the seeds and the roots. If nothing else, this book is proof that despite everything, I lived.

www.ingramcontent.com/pod-product-compliance
Lightning Source LLC
LaVergne TN
LVHW091311080426
835510LV00007B/467